GOD IN OUR LIVES

by Reverend Garry A. Scheuer, Jr.

The C. R. Gibson Company
Norwalk, Connecticut

CONTENTS

INTRODUCTION

Just before the night ends and the day begins, there is a time when we know that the darkness is going and the light is coming. We call it dawn. Suddenly it is daytime. Light dawns! It is born in the process of change — from death to life, from sadness to joy, from hate to love.

There are people who are aware of God and those who are unaware of God. There are people moving toward God and people moving away from God. This book offers brief glimpses from actual experience to show how those who were unaware gained awareness; how those who were moving away began to move toward God. These are stories of that powerful instant between darkness and daylight which is the dawn of the Spirit.

— Garry A. Scheuer, Jr.

5

THE THIEF'S CHRIST

The church secretary ushered the young man into the pastor's study. She seemed hesitant as she said, "Reverend, this young man . . . has brought a . . . gift, a gift for the church, he says. He wouldn't tell me his name."

"Thank you, Ruby," the pastor said smiling. The young man was well-bearded and ill-clothed. He carried a large flat package wrapped in newspapers and tape, maybe three by five feet in size. Near the top, several bronze spikes had stabbed through the wrapping. Reverend Barrett extended his hand and shook the young man's hand. "My name is Clay Barrett . . . " The sentence hung in the air for a moment, but the young man did not introduce himself. He simply said, "I have a gift for the church."

Reverend Barrett motioned for the young man to sit down. He assumed the young man needed money and wanted to sell whatever was in the package. However, the young man repeated, "I have a gift for the church."

"What is it?" the pastor asked, and with that the visitor ripped off the newspapers. The pastor let out an audible gasp. Mounted on a wood facing and frame was a hammered-copper head of Christ. The bronze spikes that had come through the wrapping were part of the crown of thorns. It was a profile of Jesus done in deep relief, His expression conveying a sense of power and suffering. The face had a gentleness about it yet still seemed to look firm and resolute.

The pastor was silent for a long time. Then he said, "It's strong and beautiful! Where did you get this piece of art work?" The young man held out his hands and said, "From these."

"Are you a sculptor?" the pastor guessed.

The young man gave a quick smile and said, "No, not by a long shot. I'm an apprentice in sheet metal work. My boss does some pretty fancy stuff, decorative work in copper — things like that. He let me have the copper to make this head of Christ. I'm interested in art and . . . well, someday I'd like to be able to answer your question with a 'yes, I am a sculptor!' "

Pastor Barrett sat back in his chair. He looked at the copper head of Christ. The strong features, the realistic crown of thorns, the hair that fell to the shoulder much like that of the young man who had created this Christ. "How much do you want for the piece?" the pastor said directly.

The young man shook his head. "You don't understand. Like your secretary said, I want to give it to the church as a gift."

"But just the materials alone were costly. Your time and effort and talent are invaluable. Why would you want to give it away?" The pastor was genuinely puzzled.

"I just want to make a gift to your church! A gift — no strings attached." The young man seemed upset now. "I don't want any money for it," he said firmly.

The pastor sensed that there was something more to this matter than a simple gift. He said, "You haven't told me your name."

The youth shook his head and said nothing.

"Are you from the community here?" the pastor asked.

"No," he replied, "no, look — if this isn't good enough for the church . . . I just want to give it to the church as a gift!" Now the young man seemed desperate. "Please just accept it and don't ask questions."

Clay Barrett wanted to respect the request. Still his experience told him that people who were in trouble often had difficulty talking about it. Intuition said, "This man needs help!" He decided to risk additional questions. "I don't know your church background though I suspect you wouldn't be fashioning heads of Christ unless you were a Christian. Is that true?" He knew the young man might refuse to answer or worse yet might leave. But he felt the pressure of concern. Already he felt the demand of the Love of Christ that always seemed to say, "Comfort my people."

"Yes, it's true. I am a Christian — a Roman Catholic."

Now Pastor Barrett did react with surprise. "Then why are you bearing this beautiful gift to a Protestant Church? Why not to the Catholic Church down the street?"

The young man was firm — "I can't tell you!" He seemed troubled, almost fearful.

"Anything you say to me will be held in strictest confidence," the pastor said. "It usually helps to talk a situation through. I don't have any idea what you need to talk about, but whatever it is our sharing of it can ease your mind. I am simply concerned and want to help if I can."

The two men sat in silence for a short period that seemed very long and threatened to grow longer. Finally the youth spoke with a shrug, "My name is John Wellston." With that he stood up and stepped toward the pastor extending his hand. They shook hands in a mildly formal manner. John seemed to be satisfied with that and sat down.

He took a deep breath and said, "It's a long story. It goes way back to when I was 13 years old. I'm 27 now. Back then there was a gang of boys here in this neighborhood. I was one of them. In fact, I guess you'd say I was sort of a leader. There were six of us and we were always together. We thought we were pretty tough. We smoked and stole beer from our dads. We would meet back of this church behind the storage shed in the summer time and drink the beer. One of the guys did some shoplifting at the dime store and got away with it. I don't even know how we made the transition, but pretty soon we were breaking into a house where no one was home and then into a store to steal stuff we couldn't buy like liquor and cigarettes. One night we were out back of the church and someone saw an open window at the back of the building. None of us went to church and none of us knew or cared that it was Easter eve. We got the window open and went inside." John paused, obviously somewhat embarrassed.

Pastor Barrett nodded. "That was a long time before I came here. I must have heard the story from a dozen members of the church. Go on, John."

"Well, we got to fooling around. Like you say, you've heard about it. We dumped over book cases and messed up some classrooms in the Sunday School. Then we went into the sanctuary. We tore the microphones off the lectern and pulpit. We knew we could sell those. The street light outside lighted the sanctuary and made the cross on the altar glisten in the dim darkness. One of the boys saw it and we decided to take it." At this point John bowed his head. He was silent for a minute then he went on without raising his head. "We took all the things to the window and out. We ran down the alley and then to Phil's house. We knew his folks were gone. When we got there we were all scared stiff. One of the guys said, 'What will we do with that cross? We can't sell it. We can't use it and we can't risk hiding it.' We decided to ditch it. We tossed it into a storm sewer."

John seemed to want to be silent for a moment. Pastor Barrett waited. Finally he said, "John, that still doesn't explain the head of Christ."

"I know. That comes later. Anyway, we committed some other crimes after that. We never did get caught. As we got older, we split up and I just drifted. I had quit high school. I had a job as a clerk in a men's store, as a construction worker and as a delivery driver for a drug store. I met a girl and she loved me. Life seems different if you are loved or if you love someone. She is a Christian, a Roman Catholic. I went to church with her. At first because I loved her. I go now because I love God." John was sitting up straighter now and looking directly at Pastor Barrett.

"Do you know about confession?" he asked.

"Yes, I do. We have a little different way of doing it," the pastor said, "but I know of your church's practice."

"Well, when I finally decided to join the church I was prepared to go all the way. I mean I had been 'nothing' for so long and now I had a wife. We wanted a family, too. I had started my apprenticeship with Jack's company and was developing my interest in art. It all fit together."

"I'd say you were pretty fortunate," the pastor remarked.

"That's what Father Johnston said. I agree! Anyway, I went all the way with the Roman Catholic faith. I am very regular at mass. My wife and I are involved in several projects in church. We give regularly to support the church. We belong to a study group and practice prayer and devotions in our home and we go to confession."

"It sounds like you have developed a solid Christian faith," Pastor Barrett said with real admiration.

"True, and still I felt up tight about life and about myself. Anyway, one day when I went to confession it came to me. The crime against your church. I had actually been the one to carry the cross out of the church. I thought of that dark night, of the light on the cross, of the smooth cool metal in my hands. None of it had meant anything to me then."

"As I entered the confessional and began to speak, the whole story poured out. I can tell it easily now. The first time though I was shaking like a leaf. Then by the time I had finished I was already feeling relief and a lifting of the pressure."

Reverend Barrett remained silent as John paused. He did not want to interrupt as the young man concluded his story.

John resumed, "The priest said to make restitution for the crime against the church. I don't know how much the cross and other things cost, but we've got no left-over money. To be truthful, we're broke. So I got the materials from my boss when I explained I wanted to make a gift for the church. Thank God, he didn't ask any questions. I made the Head of Christ and here it is. Will you accept it as restitution for the robbery and damages?"

Clay Barrett felt the Spirit of Christ alive in the room as he looked at the young man and at the copper head of Christ. "We are honored to have such a work of art. I have only one request. I will not reveal your identity, but please let me tell your story so others will know."

John thought about it. Then he answered carefully, "If you think it will help someone to hear the story, then tell it."

EPILOGUE

The names of people and places have been changed to protect 'John' and to keep faith with a promise. But the Head of Christ, the Thief's Christ, really exists. It hangs in the church that had been robbed and then repaid. The Head of Christ has served many times as the basis of a sermon or meditation. It has appeared before many groups and assemblies to witness to the redeeming power of the Spirit of the Christ portrays. And — 'John'? Yes, he's a sculptor!

THE GOOD SAMARITANS

The sound of the organ playing merged with the sound of the Atlantic surf in the small resort town church. The service was more than half over when the pastor made several announcements, including one concerning a meeting to be held that evening.

Several pastors and lay-leaders of churches in the area, he said, were deeply concerned with the problem created in the summer by youth who migrated to the area in large numbers and caused great distress among local citizens and business men. The quiet resort area was literally flooded by the young people from the beginning to the end of the summer.

The pastor was about to resume the service when he noticed a little gray-haired woman of about seventy-five or eighty who had stood up about halfway back in the congregation. She was waving her hand like a school child with the answer to a teacher's question. Almost without thinking the pastor, like a schoolteacher, pointed to her and said, "Yes, Mrs. Bloom, what is it?"

She coughed once, holding the pew for support, then she spoke in a soft, cultured voice that indicated the quality of of the speaker. This was what she said, "Reverend, church members and guests, I am sorry to interrupt the service in this manner but I feel that what I have to say must be told here and now. The Reverend referred to the young people who have flocked to our area and to our town. Most citizens call them the 'youth problem'. "

She waited, as if to gain breath and strength. Then she spoke again. The congregation sat in absolute silence.

"I used that phrase, too. I feared these young people. Their dress is so strange and their behavior so different. I have doubled the locks on my doors and I have had floodlights placed about my yard."

"Last week, as some of you know, I had a terrible accident driving my car on the highway. I became dizzy and fainted. I shall drive no more now, for I swerved off the road and collided with a tree. I'm afraid I constitute a hazard to navigation. At any rate, I lay unconscious for several minutes. Mind you, I was in clear sight of the highway and no one stopped to help or even inquire of my need."

"When I came to, I tried to get out of the automobile. I took only about four steps and collapsed beside the road. As I awoke again, I heard footsteps and laughter. I could see from where I lay that a group of young people were coming toward me. There were five of them, four young men and one girl. They looked terrible. They were dusty from the road. Their clothes were old and torn. Their hair was long and unkempt. I knew for certain they would rob me and I feared for my life."

She paused now and people began to fidget in their seats. In the back of the church someone whispered something, but two or three people responded with "shhh!"

The lady went on with obvious emotion. "Those young people bent over me. One took off an old army coat and put it over me. One of the boys held my hand and the young lady took water from a canteen she was carrying to bathe my forehead. Another boy backed my automobile away from the tree and parked it straight and off the road. The other young man had run off down the highway. He went to the filling station by Jackson's Crossing and called for an ambulance. They brought my car along to the hospital. Two of them waited for me. They then drove me home after my arm was bandaged. The doctor had given me medication and the young lady saw that I was comfortable on my sofa. They refused money for their kind help and only after much persuasion was I able to get more than their first names. I insisted I wanted to write their parents to indicate my deep gratitude. I have done so.

"At my insistence, they had sandwiches and then they left the house. I must admit they left my home a little more tidy than they had found it.

"Believe me when I say I am concerned for young people — for those who stopped and all the others. I'm concerned because they are so human and so much in need. I shall offer up to $5,000.00 giving one dollar for each collected by the churches to help fund an active program of concern for these young people. I hope some of you will come to the meeting tonight. Perhaps you have some thoughts on how we can help our younger brothers and sisters."

With that she sat down. The pastor smiled at the congregation. "The Lord is in His holy temple, let us keep silence before Him." They bowed in silent prayer. The pastor concluded it by saying, "Bless us, O Lord, as your word comes alive and the streets and highways of our town become the road to Jericho or to Damascus. Remind us again and again there are "good" Samaritans. In Jesus' name, Amen." "And now, Thelma," he said to the organist, "play the closing hymn loud and clear. Everybody sing!"

And the rafters of the church echoed with song!

MORE THAN ONE ROOMMATE

The hospital room held two beds. Mrs. Frank was in one of them, a heavy woman suffering from a severely infected foot and gangrene. Her pastor, Mr. Williams, stood at the door. He had made a point to see her since her husband had called to say that in all likelihood they would have to amputate her leg. In the other bed was a woman who was recovering from major surgery.

The pastor spoke with both women and then sat down to talk at length with Mrs. Frank. He spoke words of comfort and strength to help her see beyond the difficult operation and loss she must endure. They talked about the years of her faith and the willing service she had given the church, about her husband's retirement and her son who was away at college. After a while, the pastor said, "Let's pray, Emma!" The prayer was for strength and help, for the blessing of God's Spirit in this painful situation. The prayer witnessed to the healing power of God and sought to comfort the woman so she might find peace in the midst of her trouble.

When the prayer had ended, the woman in the next bed, who had reverently bowed her head during the prayer,

19

asked shyly if she might add her own prayer. She said, "My name is Eileen," and she again bowed her head and prayed, "Dear God, this lady is your servant and she is in need of healing and health — grant her that healing so she can serve you — in Jesus' name, Amen!"

Several days later Mr. Frank called the pastor to tell him that the infection had responded completely to treatment and the operation — first temporarily delayed — had been finally canceled.

When the pastor saw Mrs. Frank at home several days later, she said, "I have a thousand questions and no answers. That lady, Eileen, prayed for healing and after that I got better and better." The pastor, Mr. Williams, was silent for a moment. Then he said, "God works in our lives and we know one thing for sure — God's power is forever beyond the most radical extent of our faith and prayer. Trusting in Christ we may dare to knock on every door. We can hope for the very best — for the miracle — even as we seek His help and support and strength to endure the very worst, Emma. God is always with us and where He is anything can happen."

Mrs. Frank smiled, "I guess I had more than one roommate!"

SPLIT SECOND FAITH

There was an explosive crack of metal hitting metal at high speed.

Woody Hubbert was at the wheel of his station wagon pulling their camper-trailer. His wife was reading in the seat next to him. Their six children were seated and stretched out around the second seat and rear of the wagon.

Traveling at the speed limit, Woody maneuvered to pass two semi-trailer trucks that were in the right lane one right after the other. He eased out and passed the one truck. He was beside the second truck when the driver, possibly falling asleep, caused the truck to start over into the left lane. Woody hit the brakes and went onto the shoulder. They were traveling downhill on the highway and beyond the shoulder was a fearsome dropoff of thirty or forty feet. He fought for control of the car and regained the road in time to thread his way through between a bridge rail and the back of the rear truck. The travel-trailer fishtailed and struck the rear wheel of the truck bounding off of it and forcing the car to the shoulder again. Woody struggled with the wheel as the tires alternated on gravel, grass and concrete.

The two youngest children were crying by the time Woody brought the car to a standstill. Their ten-year old had a bump on her forehead and their fourteen-year-old had banged his elbow against the window handle. Everybody was talking at once. All of the comments were sounds of relief and the release of tension that the split second of terror was ended. Woody sat back with a sigh. Coincidentally, there was no traffic on the highway at this moment. Everyone was still for an instant. No one spoke. The silence was not heavy nor like a break in reality. Instead, the silence was light and happy. Relief! Gratitude! A heavy sigh to quiet the nerves.

Woody turned to his wife. "Mag, I didn't think we were going to make it." He concentrated on his thoughts for a time. "Honey, in the midst of all that noise and confusion, I can only remember three words we spoke, 'God help us!' I heard them twice. I don't even know for sure who spoke those words. I know the thought went through my mind at the time that if we were really going to crash, we would want to know and acknowledge His love, especially in that split second. In a way, all of our faith was packed into that second or two. If it can't hold there it can't hold anywhere."

His wife nodded, "I think I said 'God help us' and I think you did. Anyway, I had a reaction to the words and some thoughts went through my head, too. I felt myself relax. I think the impulse to scream died in my brain without being sent out. I trust your driving ability. It never occurred to me to ask God to handle the driving, but I had a feeling that should the driving end right here in death or injury that we could have left everything else to God. We could ask Him to handle it all."

Woody laughed, relaxed now, with his wife's words. "While we're sitting here . . . maybe . . . children, Honey . . . we could take time for a little prayer of gratitude and thanksgiving . . . after I check the trailer and the car." He climbed out and walked a circle around the vehicles.

It was the Hubbert's custom to have a prayer for safety for themselves and others as they left their house for a trip, and to have a prayer of thanks when they returned. Now, as Woody climbed back into the car, on the silent road, they bowed their heads and Woody said, "God we pray all the time . . . not so we can be careless and still safe, but so we will be alert. We thank you for the feeling of assurance and for your Spirit present with us in that terrible moment. Be with us now for the rest of the trip and in your grace and power be with every driver whatever happens. In Jesus' name, Amen."

Margaret said "Amen" and the children echoed, "Amen, Amen." The rush of traffic resumed and Woody pulled off the shoulder and into the stream of cars and trucks humming, "King of the Road."

PUT YOUR HAND IN THE HAND

The rock gave way and Phil dropped straight down the sheer face of the mountain. As he slammed against the cold rock everything went black. The four men were experienced climbers. Phil and Wayne had spent years climbing. They were careful and well organized. Pat and Butch were younger and not as experienced but were extremely strong and capable.

Each year now for three years the men had climbed as a team. They were so good that all but the most difficult climbs seemed routine. Still they practiced and trained. They prepared carefully and worked with deliberate caution and deep concentration. They had set out on the third year studying two or three major ascents, planning to choose one for the summer. They were doing rock cliffs to improve their technique and communications.

Phil's fall was their first serious mishap. He hung there now, unconscious. Blood ran down the face of the cliff. He was suspended two hundred and fifty yards above a safe ledge and four hundred yards from the ground below. All four of the men had lived close to nature for most of their lives.

They knew the dangers in what they were doing. They had a natural faith, born of a closeness to God's creation, though they lacked any regular or formal expression of that faith. Their climbing itself seemed like a religious affirmation.

Now as they worked around the sheer rock to reach Phil, they were stunned by the sight of his body. Wayne dispatched Pat to descend and get help while he and Butch tried to lower Phil to the ground. As they were transferring his gear, Phil came to. He was in great pain. When they tried to move him, his reaction brought his safety rope over a sharp edge and cut him free from Wayne. Butch's rope, just attached, still held but Phil was about to fall another fifteen feet or more down the cliff. Wayne, closest to him, made a desperate grab and their hands locked, each gripping the other's wrist. An eternity passed as Butch worked his way back to help. Phil opened his eyes to look into Wayne's eyes. No rope held them together, just the firm bond of hand on wrist interlocked.

Phil sensed very slowly where he was and what was happening. He had no way of knowing that the rope was still fastened to Butch. Nor did it matter. Fear crossed his eyes. The two men looked at one another — face to face. Phil seemed to relax yet he tightened his grip. Wayne held on and waited for the telltale slippage that would indicate Phil was losing consciousness. Wayne knew he couldn't hold much longer.

Butch was just a step or two away now. "You're still tied on to Butch," Wayne said. Phil didn't respond. As Butch reached him and the two men made him secure with new ropes,

Phil went limp, his fierce grip relaxing.

When Wayne and Butch reached the road, Pat was waiting with an ambulance. They placed Phil carefully into the rear of the ambulance and Wayne checked to see that he was all right. He looked at Wayne and said, "The man was with us!" Then he was gone.

Two days later Wayne, Butch and Pat went to visit Phil at the little county hospital. They joshed and kidded the nurse in charge until she let them in to see Phil. His head was bandaged. He had two black eyes and his nose was cut and bruised. Otherwise he looked very much alive.

"How're you doing?" — the three visitors all spoke at once. "I'm fine, really fine," Phil said, "couldn't be better!" Wayne looked at his injured friend and Pat and Butch. Turning back to Phil on the bed, he said, "What have you got going in that scrambled brain of yours, fella? What's going on?"

Phil looked from one man to the other. "Up there, on the cliff, it really happened. I was about to die, to give up, and God reached out to help me."

Wayne laughed, "Thanks a lot for the top billing, but that was only me." Phil laughed, too, but shook his head. "I know it was your hand. But, I was praying. I didn't want to drag anyone down with me. And I heard that song *Put Your Hand in the Hand of the Man from Galilee.* I was half conscious. I don't even like the song. It was more like a background. I guess I remembered it because my hand was in yours and my life depended on it. Anyway, through all these thoughts one clear and simple thing happened. I heard . . . no, felt . . . the words 'Trust me!' " Phil rested a minute. The other three men looked at each other and shrugged. "I remembered a Sunday School picture of a lamb hung up on a ledge with Jesus, the Good Shepherd, reaching down to save the lamb. I felt real strength flowing through my body. I felt really calm and confident. That was it! Butch reached me and the next thing I remember is this ceiling and that cute little nurse standing over me with a hypodermic needle." Phil relaxed.

Wayne walked to the windows and looked out at the mountains in the distance. "I felt that strength, Phil. I actually did. And when you were in the ambulance you said, 'The man was with us.' "

Butch stepped to the bed. "You were hit right in the head, man. You were dreaming. Your reactions took over." "Sure," Pat put in, "anyone would get a little shook up with a bop like that."

"I agree," Phil said, "but this was different — real — a simple, solid thing. Wayne, hand me that Bible off of the dresser." Wayne handed the book to Phil, who lifted himself with some difficulty and opened the pages. "Read this right here." Wayne took the book and read to himself. He went back and read it aloud, "I am with you always."

"And He is," said Phil.

THE SEARCH

Roland Mason woke to a sense of unreality. "Today is the day!" Today he would graduate from seminary as a minister in the Church. The fact that he was forty-seven years old did nothing to decrease his excitement for this day. Once or twice during his three years at the seminary, Roland had looked around at the young men and women there and asked himself, "What's an old guy like you doing in a place like this?" Married and father of two teenage young people, Roland many years the senior of the other members of his graduating class. And, strangely enough, the uniqueness of his age the least of his story. "Now! Today is the day!"

As he got out of bed, he said to himself, "Make a joyful noise unto God, all ye lands; Sing forth the honor of His name, make His praise glorious." He revelled in the scripture. Scenes of ancient Israel and of futuristic rockets beyond the orbit of Pluto drifted through his active mind. "Today is the day!"

He put on the coffee and called his wife. "Anne! Anne! for crying out loud, it's graduation day!" He laughed when

he heard her moan. She always moaned in the
He would tell her, "You don't know the difference
morning and mourning." She always laughed.
her morning moan was traitor to the real love for
creation that lived in her heart. Once awake, Anne
siasm and joy were seldom matched by Roland, eve
best. Today was no different. She bounded out
and around their seminary apartment talking e
about details. She spoke of the members of the fami
ing for the graduation ceremony, the preparation
land's address on behalf of the class — they had
unanimously asking him to speak for their faith
dreams, their aspirations. He had told Annie, with
"They see me as a father-figure." But she said, "Th
you as a leader with common sense and a good se
humor."

Today she bubbled. His suit was pressed! The roas
ready! Their two girls would be back from the slu
party by noon. Roland's brother would bring their r
"Everybody's going to be there except old Sna
our dog."

Partly because of Anne's enthusiasm and partly in spi
it, Roland was ready when the ceremony began. The
had been a whirl of congratulations and more food t
twice that many people would have needed to surv

The organ in the great sanctuary swelled to magnifice
and dropped away to silence. After the processional, t
class stood motionless for an instant and then, as practice
they sat down together at the front of the crowded churc

As was the custom of the seminary, the graduation was held in town at a large local church — a community gesture and a concession to practicality. The seminary chapel couldn't hold the crowd.

As they sat down and the ceremony continued, Roland looked with genuine love and admiration at the men and women in his class. He was proud to be one of them. He began to think back beyond college, to his earlier life.

"You'll blow up the house with all those chemicals," his father said. Roland was a searcher, an experimenter. The other kids in high school called him "the brain". He never worried much about what they called him and wouldn't even have known about it if a friend hadn't told him. He just accepted it. Anyway, he graduated in three years and had to decide from which of several colleges he would accept a scholarship. He went into chemistry, but switched to nuclear physics. He was just twenty when he entered graduate school and only twenty-four when he secured his doctorate. At twenty-six he had patents on three of his inventions, including an improved laser used in delicate manufacturing processes.

Roland met Anne when he was twenty-seven. She was a librarian in the research lab's reference library. While her physical appearance helped, it was actually her astute knowledge of his field and her obvious happiness that, as he put it, " stopped me dead in my tracks!"

They courted in the lunchroom at the laboratory and while discussing research. They soon graduated to long drives

in the country on weekends and intimate conversations in a little Italian restaurant near Anne's apartment.

Anne and Roland were married by a Justice of the Peace. A friend summed it up, "Together they put more I.Q. under one roof than any ten people."

Roland, absorbed in his research, was startled to find that he was a millionaire. It hadn't really happened over night. Money came from his inventions and his partnership in several research and development projects, his high-ranked teaching position at the university, his part-ownership of a small manufacturing company that landed several space contracts, and from the publication of some of his research. Anne had become increasingly responsible for the family's financial responsibilities. One night she simply announced, "How does it feel to be rich?" Roland had to have her explain it twice. The things he had done were done for "the search", for the pleasure and thrill of discovery. He didn't resent money, he just didn't usually consider it.

Deep in his research, Roland drew away from his wife, Anne. His natural humor seemed to give way to desperation. He searched! Facts bowed before him. He mastered unknown reality and made reality out of fantasies others had only dreamed of. He hungered for knowledge — for truth.

It is ironic that it was Anne who stumbled onto "the Truth, The Way and the Life," while Roland sought to cover his frustration in other ways.

31

"We meet twice a month at the university student center," Denise had said. Anne went along. "Religion. We're not against it, we just never thought about it," was Anne's first response. In the small group at the student center, she encountered people like herself. And they had thought about it. "You shouldn't really say Anne was converted," Denise said. "That's not the way we approach it anyway." But Anne started thinking about it. The validity and value of the Gospel of Jesus Christ and the power of God alive in nature and history came home to her. The group was open and free with their thoughts and beliefs, firm in conviction, they were relaxed in acceptance of each other and of persons like Anne who came because she was lonely, because she was searching, because she was certain there had to be more to life than she knew.

"I don't care, I don't care what you say, I am a Doctor of Nuclear Physics." Roland's voice was slurred and his speech too slow. He slipped from the stool by the back of the bar. Drinking was hardly a problem for him. He had passed it over for a narcotic addiction that gripped him solid in its iron fist. He was in the bar to meet the man who supplied his need. He didn't care how he had gotten started. If he did he would have laughed, his investigative curiosity soaked in vodka called on him to "try it!" Now it was too late. Anne knew. He recalled with some confusion she had said something about "God" and "prayer" and . . . and . . . "love." The part about love didn't confuse him so he held on to that.

He was arguing with a man who was small, about his size. But the man looked like he had pushed packing crates at the docks rather than buttons on a computer. When the police arrived, Roland was flat on the floor. Cooling off in jail, Roland resolved to buy a huge supply of the narcotics so he wouldn't have to "go downtown" every week. "Now that makes sense," he said as he fell asleep.

He lost almost everything he had. Fortunately he did not lose Anne. Somewhere around rock bottom, they got together and he took hold of what was left of his mind and body and what little he had in money and knowledge. Roland came back — not as strong, not as big, not as rich — but a lot smarter. "From the bottom of things, the perspective is pretty clear and pretty simple. Up is the way out. And you *don't make it alone!* At the bottom — that's where I learned to pray . . . at the bottom. Being on my knees was a step up for me. It was 'up' from lying face down in my own shame."

"As I got respectable, I realized I could do it all over again. But I asked, 'Why?' I started to look around. I had been 'gone' from the world and it didn't matter. The world went on. I looked around, from sub-atomic structures to the furthest star and only one thing made any sense. When I was all the way down, I was loved. Anne had been there but more than that the 'common sense Christians' of her 'little bunch' were there. When I stood on my own two feet again they cheered. When I went back to work, they had a 'milk and sandwich' party for me. One of them said, 'a disgustingly simple bill of fare, but it's the company that counts.' We could laugh together."

Sitting at the graduation exercises, Roland recalled vividly that no one laughed when he said he was going into the ministry. They had spent an evening talking about it.

The "little bunch" had raised the question of wise use of his scientific training and ability. They questioned his motives, but they didn't laugh at him and they vowed to support him in whatever he decided.

He turned in his seat to look past the rows of graduates to the pew where the "little bunch" sat now. One of the men in the group clenched his fist and raised it high enough for Roland to see. Then he gave it an affirming shake as he nodded.

" . . . and by unanimous choice of the student body . . . " Roland braced himself ". . . it is my pleasure to present him his diploma as I present him to you, soon to be the Reverend Doctor Roland . . ." Roland stood and made his way to the lectern in the chancel. All his life he had searched for truth, for fulfillment. As he grasped the diploma, he realized this was not the completion of his search, but the beginning. The difference — the real difference — was that now he did not search alone, nor in vain. He faced the student body and congregation and he began his speech, "We are not alone! . . . "

HER FAITH BEGAN IN DARKNESS

Her name is Edna. She starts her story by saying, "My faith really began underground." She continues, obviously happy with her faith, wherever it began. "The whole thing goes back to when we were travelling, camping." Her husband likes to camp because it "throws us together as a family." Edna chuckles about that, "we have five children — it seems to me we're thrown together most of the time."

Edna's enthusiasm is contagious. She is about 28 or 29 now, but when she speaks of her faith or her family there is an almost childish excitement. Her smile is broad and benevolent — coming quickly — staying persistently — and shining on anyone who happens to be present.

"We usually drive about 200 or 300 miles a day, but in order to make the state park where we wanted to camp, we pressed on to make over 400 miles that day." She wrinkles her nose. "We were a mess. The kids were dirty and tired. We were hungry. The tent was still wet from the last place we stayed and my patience was just as soggy."

They were camping in the midwest where, among woods and streams, there are great natural caverns. They had "pressed" to get to the certain camp grounds so the next day they could tour the caves.

Edna goes on, "The next morning we were all up at dawn, refreshed and ready to go. I love breakfast when we camp because my husband cooks it!" she comments.

The family cleaned up after breakfast — Edna's husband who had done most of the driving decided to get some additional sleep. Edna and the children, ages 2 to 11, hiked to the cave site. It was a week day and at first they were the only ones there. The guide, a weathered middle-aged man in work pants and laced boots, sold them a cave tour ticket. Then he tore each ticket in half. One of the boys remarked, "Gee, just like the movies, Mom!" The guide chuckled and chatted with them. The cave and its history came alive and the children, one by one, became interested. "All except little Jammy," Edna recalls, "he was rarely interested in anything when he was two except his "ba-ba" — that's his bottle, his blanket, his 'big truck' ".

The guide lighted his gas lantern and was just about to start the tour for the family when four young men pulled up in a car and jumped out. They bought tour tickets from the guide, paying little attention to Edna or her family. The young men were loud — pushing each other and joking. They talked softly among themselves and laughed loud and long. The cave guide was obviously irritated by them, but he started the tour.

"I don't have to tell you that we were uncomfortable from the start and it wasn't too long before we were scared," Edna says seriously. "As those boys jostled each other, their language became more abusive and their laughter louder and louder." The guide carried the only light and the shadows closed in around the tour group. The guide's voice droned through his talk — the boys' rude joking rising and falling.

"I had the children gathered around me like chicks around a mother hen. We came to the central cavern — a huge domed room over 200 feet across and 50 feet high. The children had picked up my fear by now," Edna admits.

The guide led the group to the center of the cavern where he asked they be seated on some wooden benches. The four young men started fighting playfully over one of the benches.

The guide explained the large room, its underground stream and rock formations. He kept looking with apology at Edna. He was seriously troubled with the way the young men were acting. He, too, seemed afraid. Then he said, "Underground here there are no light sources except our lantern and the emergency lighting system. Ma'am, be sure you have hold of all your children. I'll turn off my lantern so we can get a feeling for complete darkness, then I'll light a single match so you can see what even the tiniest light will do in that darkness." With those words the cavern went black as the knob on the lantern squeaked and the steady hiss of the gas stopped.

"The whole group went silent. The black darkness blotted

out our sight, but more than that, it seemed to strike physically, to press down on us, to squeeze my thumping heart," Edna says. Her smile is not quite as quick and easy now. The memory of the moment returns in strength.

"One of the children started to cry. Then I realized in the confusion of my fear, Jammy was out of touch. He was not afraid of darkness. I called out, 'Jammy!' " Now Edna's smile is gone, lost in the reality of the story. "I knew the guide was about to light the match," she says, "I heard the scratch and light flared." Jammy had wandered away and was walking straight for the underground stream. "I screamed and started toward him," Edna says, "but I saw a movement out of the corner of my eye and just then the guide lit the gas lantern. The cavern was flooded with light. One of the young men had launched off the bench and was racing for Jammy. He scooped him up in his arms just a few feet short of the rail near the underground stream." Now Edna is able to grin again as she says, "I sat there looking at that smiling young man carrying my baby back to me and I heard his friends and my children let out a genuine cheer. I thought of John's words in his Gospel, 'The light shines in the darkness, and the darkness has not overcome it.' My silly fears died in the light of that little match and the flare of the lantern. I found a new faith in God and in my fellow human beings. I'd always been a Christian, for as long as I could remember. But my faith really began there underground in the blackness of that cavern and with the coming of light — light of all kinds."

CHILD OF HOPE

It was a typical Indianapolis summer rain. Clouds swept swiftly over the moon and stars. Distant lightning crackled suddenly overhead and the rain fell in thick sheets that drenched everything in its path.

Timmy, a high school freshman, wouldn't have worn a raincoat even if he had known it was going to rain. As he came out of the supermarket with the two gallons of milk in a sack under his arm, he was soaked before he reached his bike. Strapping the milk onto the carrier, back of the seat, he ducked his head and pedaled furiously for home. In that area of town there are no sidewalks or curbs and he had to ride alternately on the gravel shoulder, through mud puddles, and onto the black asphalt.

The first car to hit him only sideswiped his rear wheel. Off balance, half-blinded by the rain, confused by the sudden noise and the impact of the car, Timmy struggled for control of his bike. He crossed the center line on the road and was struck head-on by a truck. He was knocked back across the center line into the oncoming traffic and hit by two cars before the man from the first car could reach him and halt traffic long enough to drag him off the road.

The ambulance light rotating in the rain bounced red off of everything in sight. The white-clothed driver of the ambulance shook his head as he closed the back door of the vehicle. Timmy lay inside strapped to the stretcher and an attendant sat right beside him. But the driver's face told the story. There was really no hope!

In intensive care, doctors and nurses worked around the clock to preserve the little flickering spark of life in Timmy's crushed and broken body. Repeatedly, the doctors used the phrase "little or no hope". Timmy's parents had no frame of reference to use in understanding Timmy's condition. He had hardly ever been sick. He had lived almost accident-free. He played basketball and baseball at school and was constantly "working out". The doctors pointed out that given less than his near-perfect physical condition, Timmy would have been dead already.

Everything that could be done medically was done. His condition stabilized at "poor" and Timmy lay silent and unmoving on his hospital bed.

Trudy was a nurse who did private duty. Timmy's parents hired her as much out of frustration as anything. They just couldn't think of any other contribution to make to their son's hopeless condition. It seemed as if they were "doing something" by having the nurse on duty. Trudy lived on the same side of Indianapolis as Timmy and his parents and by coincidence went to the same church. She had met the parents at services and knew Timmy because he sang in the youth choir. She came on duty with little to do but see to the details of Timmy's care. But Trudy was more than a competent nurse. She was also a highly competent Christian. She believed in prayer and used it. In the hours she was beside Timmy, she prayed for his health and welfare. She prayed for God's will to be fulfilled. She prayed, "Lord, let the power of your Spirit provide the strength and comfort we as human beings cannot give Timmy in his desperate need." She would take Timmy's hand and pray for him though he never moved or opened his eyes.

Trudy was realistic. She had worked hundreds of hours with patients of all kinds. She had gone through the feelings of doubt that come to those who care for terminal patients. She had made her peace with God in the face of faith expressed by persons who were suffering and dying. She saw the strong positive power of God alive in people whose life was lost and all but gone. So Trudy prayed, able to accept and acknowledge the love and wisdom of God, no matter what happened! When she talked about her faith — and sometimes people would ask her — she would say, "I've never seen a single person whose health was aided by the absence of prayer nor one whose health was hindered by the presence of prayer. On the contrary, I've seen many people who were helped by the presence of prayer. So I pray!"

One morning Timmy opened his eyes. He didn't speak until nine days later. When he did, they thought he said, "Can I have a coke?" Even then, common sense and medical fact said that now, though he would live, he would never walk again nor was his mind, voice or body ever likely to function at normal capacity. Honesty and integrity compelled the use of the words "little or no hope".

Still, Timmy was alive! Trudy now practically "one of the family", on her days off and on some shifts when she wasn't working, would often visit Timmy or his parents. She became a living symbol of the call to "pray without ceasing". Her prayers effected a sense of peace and a calm feeling of God's concern in Timmy's parents. For Timmy, who seemed to hear and understand Trudy better than he heard anyone else, her faith and concern apparently meant peace and rest. Later Timmy was to reveal that they meant strength and power, too.

When Timmy began to remember, he could recall only that his back wheel had been hit. The blinding flashes of pain mingled with blinding flashes of light and his mind said, "No." Everything was closed out. He was like a man trapped in a deep pit. Unconsciousness seldom yielded to sight, sound or touch. But Timmy was a fighter. He didn't know what he was fighting for or against. He just hung on to life with fierce determination and waited. Far beyond what might be expected for his teen-age years, a strong patience emerged.

He said much later, "I knew, just knew more and more, that if I held on and waited things would work out." It helped when he began to hear. The first words he heard were part of a quiet sentence that he remembered as " . . . and Lord keep the life within him strong until . . . "

He had tried to speak many times and was startled at the sound of his own voice when it said, "Can I have a coke?"

He was startled because he'd wanted to say so much more and couldn't. A tear had formed in his eye but no one noticed. It had come, not from "crying" but from the struggle and the agony of willing to speak when voice and mind refused to be coordinated.

Timmy became more and more aware of Trudy and his parents. His struggle for life responded to her attitude of prayer and faith. When he could finally talk, he had a million questions. But Timmy never asked if there was hope for him. As he came alive in his hospital bed, he was a child of hope.

"Our hope in God, in Jesus Christ, is not based on physical recovery alone or even on the preservation of our present life," Trudy said. Timmy had asked her how she would have felt if he had died after all her prayers. It was the kind of question Timmy asked now. He and Trudy were walking back from the drugstore. She had been to supper at their home and the warm summer evening had invited them to walk. She had challenged him with, "If you can make it to the drugstore, I'll buy the ice cream." Timmy used a cane to walk, but he could stand alone. As they returned from the drugstore, he told her about his disappointment because he had gotten a "B" on his last biology test. "Timmy, you don't have to get 'A's' in everything. Relax!" He shook his head with stubborn determination and said, "I can hope, can't I?"

HIS FIRST AND BEST FRIEND

Friendship as a way of life begins with one friend. Like the longest walk that begins with a single step, the first friend may be the most difficult. Many people grow up never having developed the skills involved in true friendship. Friendship involves trust and sharing — honesty and truth. But where can a person begin?

Ed stared into what was left of his cup of coffee. The babble of voices around him in the snack-shop was anonymous. It helped reinforce his mood. Ed was lonely. He shook his head and drank the remaining coffee in a quick motion. The fact that it was stone-cold made him aware of how long he had been thinking about his problem. He sighed and bumped past the other members of the noon-time crowd. He paid for his lunch and stepped outside. The impersonal noise of the city hit him like a blast. "I don't have a single friend," he blurted out in his mind, "not a single friend!" He headed back for his office.

Ed was married and he and his wife, Alice, had three children. But he had become increasingly aware of the fact that he had no friends. He would think about it at his desk at work — he would dwell on it on the commuter train riding to and from the city. "I have people I'm attached to through work and in our neighborhood. I bowl once a week and I go to church. I even go fishing once in a while with Ted and Chick." But, passing 30 and now approaching 40, Ed began to notice how shallow his relationships were with people.

Even Alice, his wife, was not his "friend". His youngest daughter, Kathy, said he was her "buddy" — but she was only three! His two sons seemed to accept him, but Teddy, at six, seldom had anything to say, and Paul, at eight, talked a lot but never about being his father's friend.

Ed's feelings were strong. He had continued to dwell on them all day — the feeling from the lunch counter would not go away. When he finished supper, he remembered he had to have the prayer for the service club meeting downtown tomorrow.

Ed was startled by the word "friend" in the New Testament. He had picked up the Bible and was thumbing through the pages looking for an idea for his prayer. He was not a regular Bible reader but he had become mildly interested now as he scanned some of the familiar passages. Then he was stopped cold by the word "friend". The sentence said, "You are my friends . . . " It was in the 15th chapter of the Gospel of John in the New Testament.

Ed didn't move for a moment. His mind raced! "Who said that?" he was asking himself. Checking the context, he discovered it was Jesus speaking. As he sat there, the Bible suddenly updated itself. It was speaking to him. His experience was no different from that of St. Augustine's or Martin Luther's. The Scriptures came alive for him in this single passage. The words leaped out at him! "You are my friends..." They homed-in on his life and problem. Here was his first step. He had a friend — Jesus! It sounded strange. He pictured himself introducing Jesus at the bowling alley — at the boat dock — or at work. "This is my friend. His name is Jesus." Ed thought the words were familiar and then he remembered the words of the hymn, "What a Friend We Have in Jesus!"

Ed accepted the first step and began to explore the nature of friendship by learning more about his "new friend." He began to condition his responses to people in relation to the way he thought Jesus would have responded to them. Ed began to realize his full potential for friendliness. At the lunch-counter he discovered that the old man back of the counter was full of interesting stories and loved to fish.

Over the days and years that followed, the man would often ask, "Warm your coffee, Ed?" and Ed would remember that gloomy day when he realized he had no friends and how he discovered he was wrong. Time and time again, Ed told the story of his first and best friend.

SEEDS ARE FOR PLANTING

Bob is pastor of a small church in a little midwestern town. One warm, quiet and rainy Wednesday morning, he sits at his desk in the parsonage opening his mail. His wife is busy in the kitchen.

Most of the letters are advertisements for things Bob and his wife, Ann, can't afford. A few of the pieces of mail are bills. There are two notes from church members — one a thank you note for a recent baptism and one concerning plans for a pot-luck supper at church.

He picks up the one remaining letter. It is from Denver, Colorado. The name and address are unknown to him. He opens the envelope sensing the little feeling of excitement that accompanies "mysterious mail". He takes out a small piece of stationery bearing the name and trademark of a florist. The letter says:

"Dear Pastor:

Last Saturday I sat in your church and worshipped. I thought how discouraging it could be when a pastor works hard all week on his Sunday sermon and then on a hot, languid Sunday morning he can only wonder if his words are falling on fertile soil. That particular morning your message did carry with me. I have thought of it many times since.

Perhaps your efforts are somewhat like our work in the flower shop. We plant a seed and hope it will grow. More often than not it does grow.

Sincerely yours,"

Bob sits back in his chair feeling the gentle touch of God's Spirit alive in the letter.

He thinks of the flowers his wife labors over day after day. He remembers the victory garden his folks planted during World War II. He thinks of the lawn and the crabgrass he can never get rid of. He knows just what the florist meant.

"Nature demands patience," he says aloud. He leans forward to the desk and writes the words on a piece of church stationery. Under these words, he writes "So do God and people."

Bob sits up and stretches. He walks out to the kitchen. At the breakfast table, he and Ann had spoken of their discouragement about their ministry and the little church they serve. Now as he reaches the kitchen, Ann is talking on the phone, finishing baking cookies and starting lunch. He puts his arms around her waist as she hangs up the phone. "Honey, I've been thinking. We just get too anxious to see 'final' results. Seeds take time to grow — people and love take time, too."

Ann smiles at him and wipes her hands on a kitchen towel. She slips a cookie sheet full of plump little dough balls into the oven. Then she says, "I guess we sounded pretty gloomy this morning." "We sure did," Bob says, as he holds the letter out to her. "Read this!" She rubs her hands on her apron and takes the letter. She sits down and reads it carefully.

When she looks up at Bob, he is deep in thought. "You know, Ann, I had forgotten to mention to you that Mr. Wallace phoned earlier while I was at the church office. He said he's interested in that idea of a lunch program for the migrant workers' children." She laughs and says, "That's great, but I can top that! You know the new family over on Bruce Lane — the Browns — you remember, you helped him get his power mower running last week? That was Mrs. Brown on the phone just then. She wanted to know what time we had services on Sunday."

Bob takes a second handful of pecan halves that Ann is chopping for the cookies as he says, "Maybe we've planted more seeds than we know." She nods and says, "With God's help, they'll grow." Then she pokes him in the ribs and adds, "Listen, Mister, unless you've planted some pecan seeds lately, you'd better get out of my bowl of nuts!"

He beats a hasty retreat from the kitchen. The sun has come out and the rain has stopped.

UNSEEN ASSIST

Picnics are not notorious for providing dramatic religious experience, but this one was — at least for one person.

It happened years ago. "The Grove" had always been the location for the Annual School Picnic in Mortontown. The junior high school students, the high school students, their parents and their families would "start the season" with the Annual Picnic. There were all the things that go with picnics. Huge tables of food to more than fill any appetite. There were big washtubs holding blocks of ice and ice cold bottles of soft drinks. Dry ice gave off its cold mist through the seams in cardboard boxes that held the ice cream . . . "for later." Impromptu games would break out as people arrived. Someone would start hitting a softball and kids would run for the woods. Some of the men would start lining up the horseshoe pegs and throw a few horseshoes to test the distance. Pretty soon the chairman of the School Board would ring the bell borrowed from the grade school. The ding dong of the bell brought everyone rushing for the tables piled with food. One of the ministers from town would call the group to silence and then he would say grace over the meal. There was always thanks for spring and summer and for the food and for the happy joy of the picnic. When the prayer ended, the president of the senior class would lead the crowd in the Pledge of Allegiance to the Flag. The flag was always held by the chairman of the Student Council from the junior high school. When the Pledge ended, a tremendous whoop would go up from the crowd and a cheer that led the rush to the tables.

Stuffed with food, the "older folks", that is, everyone not still in high school, would settle down for conversation, cards, checkers and bingo. The young folks would run off and start the softball game that would end with the men against the boys, the men traditionally winning with that mysterious secret weapon called "experience." There were other traditions like the "Unofficial Horseshoe Pitching Contest" and the valiant hope held by the junior high students that they could beat the high schoolers in events like the sack race, the three-legged race, or the watermelon eating contest. There was a swimming hole at the wide place in Black Rock Creek near "The Grove". The coach from the high school always sat by the bank and watched the swimmers and everybody thanked him by throwing him in at the end of the day. There was a barn at the top of the hill where people went to change clothes to swim. Beyond the barn were the Black Rock Quarries. Once productive in gray granite — now they were full of water and challenge.

There was an old custom that graduating senior boys had to swim across the one called "The Big Quarry." Most of the boys ignored the tradition, or begged off because of their parents' strict orders. Still, every year some of the more foolish boys would climb down on the submerged ledge at

51

the north end and swim out to touch the rock face at the south end and swim back. The rock face of the south wall was straight up and down with no place to hold on. Here is what happened.

Jimmy, David, Rich, Edward and Howard went to the barn to change to their swim suits. "Someone will see us and stop us," David said. Edward shook his head, "No, we can go one at a time in different directions and meet at the ledge."

"Do we have to do this?" Jimmy asked. He hadn't liked it from the beginning. He was in on it because of Howard, who didn't say anything now. He just changed to his swim trunks. The boys walked out of the barn from four sides and went in roundabout ways to the ledge in the quarry. When the last boy, Rich, showed up, they all shook hands. They were obviously scared but now they were committed. The south wall looked a million miles away. The water was dark and it was true — "nobody knew how deep."

Edward said, "I'm going!" and dived in. His body hitting the water sounded like an explosion in the silence of the quarry. He was a strong swimmer and reached the south wall with ease. He started back and changed from a crawl stroke to a breast stroke. He made it to the ledge easily. Then he slipped trying to get a foothold. Howard reached out to steady him and he came up on the ledge.

Howard said, "Can't prove nothing waitin' around," and he dove in. He swam slowly but steadily over and back. "It's easy. It looks far, but it's not much farther than the distance across the swimming hole and back. And the water is calm and quiet. It's easy."

David stepped to the edge of the ledge. His dive was hesitant. His breathing on his crawl stroke was erratic and twice on the way to the south wall he choked up and had to tread water to get his breath. He touched the south wall and started back. Each stroke was a laboring effort. He raised his head out of the water. The boys were encouraging him, waving and shouting. He came forward with a combination dog-paddle and breast stroke. He was almost at the ledge now. Howard yelled, "I knew you could make it!" He reached out and Edward took his hand. He pulled him up. As he did, David slipped and both boys went into the water. Edward executed a dive over David as he fell. David's head hit the submerged edge of the ledge and as Edward came up to the surface, David went under. It all happened in a split-second.

The boys stood frozen while Edward climbed up on the ledge. He turned and realized David was gone. One of the boys screamed, "He went under!" and one whispered, "Oh, no!"

Edward shouted, "Get help!" motioning to Jimmy. As Jimmy started to run up the steep path, Edward shouted after him, "and bring a rope from the barn!"

Edward, Howard and Rich took turns diving in and could find or feel nothing. They had no idea how deep to dive. Rich was not a strong swimmer and gave up trying. Edward kept going back down while Howard guarded for him.

Rich felt a strange sense of loss and frustration. He had known David all his life. He couldn't be cut off that suddenly. He was part of life. He was young and strong and just coming alive. He was a friend. Rich opened his eyes and realized he had gone part way up the path. He stepped aside to a great bush that grew there and he fell to his knees and prayed. He was familiar with prayer. It was part of life for him, but he had never considered it seriously. He didn't understand prayer — not really. He didn't understand himself now. He knelt. He prayed. He spoke directly and to the point. He did not close his eyes. Around him everything stayed the same and yet everything was different. He said, "God, help David. Help us to find him and give him his life."

From the ledge in the quarry Rich heard Edward shout, "I touched him!"

Feet rushing past — a glimpse of rope — the splash of men hitting the water. Rich was standing on the ledge again. The men had the lifeless body of David out of the water. They laid him on the bank and began artificial respiration. The doctor arrived, puffing down the path and cussing the boys. The minister came behind him and the whole crowd ringed the north and east rims of the quarry.

Rich felt a strong sense of peace. The doctor knelt over David. The minister stood in prayer. Rich touched his hand. "I prayed, too," he said. The minister looked at him for a long time. Rich said, "David will be all right . . ."

The doctor stood up. He spoke almost at a shout, "He'll recover . . . and when he's well enough, if his dad doesn't tan his hide, I will!" And with that the doctor said, "Bring him along and be careful!"

Rich looked at the minister and said, "I actually spoke with God. He was right here. I mean I really spoke with him and he helped David. I'm sure." The minister put his arm on the boy's shoulder. "Stranger things have happened, son."

And they did. The experience Rich had at the picnic affected his entire life. Even at times of deepest doubt, in the midst of war's hell that claimed several years of Rich's life, he says, "I knew God was with me and I could trust him. When it got really tough, I would think back to that moment."

Rich lives today as a Christian whose sensitive concern and loving faith have helped many. He is still powered by the "unseen assist" that touched him as a youth.

A CROSS WITHOUT MEANING

Not many stories of faith begin in a clothing store. Larry's story does. He wears a cross all the time. Usually it is a two-inch brass cross. Sometimes he wears one of a number of other crosses he has. Everywhere he goes he wears a cross visible over his shirt, his sweater or his tie.

Larry is a Protestant pastor and parish minister serving a medium-sized church in a small town. He went shopping one day in what he calls "my pre-cross days" to buy a gift for his nephew, his godson. That's where it started.

"How about a cross, Reverend," the salesman in the little men's store said. The man knew him from contact in the community and through one of the service clubs in town. He held up one of several dozen cheap medallions. The one he held was an enlarged Maltese cross, a replica of the World War I Iron Cross. Medallions were a current fad, but now were not selling as well. The store was stuck with their stock. "It's just your thing, Reverend!" Larry laughed. "I don't need to convert the kid, I just want to give him a Christmas gift." The salesman continued his pitch. "Oh, you can give him one of these, they don't mean a damn thing!"

Larry reacted. "A cross without meaning," he said. He

looked at the heavy, cheap Maltese cross. "I'll take it, Jake!" he said. An idea was jelling in his imagination. He bought a turtleneck sweater for his nephew and finished his other shopping and errands. Now, however, his attention was on the cross.

The next day at his desk Larry recalled a small gold cross, a museum reproduction he had purchased several years ago. He took it from the desk drawer. The contrasts were clear. His sermon for Sunday, "The cross without meaning," took shape quickly.

"The cross loses its meaning when Christians are silent. The cross has a story of love and power, of faith and hope. If people know the story, even if they are not Christian, they will honor and respect the cross. A cross without meaning is a judgment on us as Christians."

On Sunday morning he had the two crosses in his hand before the service. Both had a chain to go around the neck. On an impulse, Larry put on the gold cross. It stood out in startling contrast against his black robe. As he entered the sanctuary, people in the service noticed it. A few people whispered comments to their neighbors in the pew. Other than that, the service went as usual.

For the sermon Larry held up the Iron Cross and told the story of how he happened to purchase it. He spoke of the need to recapture the meaning of the cross. "A cross without meaning means a world without hope." Finally he pointed to the cross on the chain at his neck, the museum reproduction. He said, "Since the world, represented by the clothing store salesman, no longer understands or accepts the meaning and importance of the cross, I intend to wear this cross for services every Sunday to make that point."

After the service people reacted in various ways. A teenager said, "I think it's cool." An elderly lady remembered that she had seen the original 12th century Greek cross, after which the museum reproduction was modeled, at the New York Museum where it is on display. A man said, "All the clergy are acting like hippies these days." Another man said, "The cross is our symbol, and I say good for you!"

Larry felt pretty good about his idea and the impact it had on people. The next two days several people spoke of the crosses and were interested. The sermon had made an impression.

Over the sound of the power mower, Larry heard the honk of a horn. He turned and waved. It was Phillip, a boy from the neighborhood. He only attended church occasionally but he had been there Sunday. Driving home from the grocery store where he worked, Phillip would stop and talk if Larry was out in the yard. They usually went back and forth on questions of faith and ideas about God, but they also talked about cars and boy-girl relationships, about war and education. Phillip was a searcher, open and honest about his doubts and his feelings.

As Phillip walked up he looked at Larry and said, "Where's your cross?" Larry shrugged and said, "In my desk drawer, but I'll be wearing it Sunday." Phillip looked at him for a second, then said, "You know, you're chicken, Reverend!

If you really meant what you said — really meant it — you'd wear that cross all the time!" Larry looked intently at the young man. It was obvious he was serious. "Don't think I haven't thought of that, Phil. I don't know . . . I think you're right, but I'm not sure it's my way or that it's a good thing to do. Wearing a cross all the time can say so many different things to so many different people. I could do more harm than good. Maybe . . . " His voice trailed off. Uncertain of his own feelings he changed the subject.

Two days later Phillip was killed when a truck came through a red light at an intersection and destroyed his car and his life . . . but not his idea.

Larry was never able to tell Phillip that the day after they had talked in the yard, after a long night of thought and prayer, he had decided to accept Phillip's challenge at face value. He had decided to wear the cross at all times, no matter what. That was years ago. Day by day the cross has provided a point of contact with countless people. "What does that mean?" they will ask. "Why are you wearing that?" they ask.

Some people have strong or unusual reactions. Larry has been called a "Commie," a "show off," and a "radical" for wearing the cross. Some people joke about it and some are very seriously and deeply moved. Day by day Larry has been able to give meaning to the cross and to people's life and faith.

Even "the cross without meaning" served its Lord.

THROUGH THE VALLEY OF THE SHADOW

The cruel words didn't go with the soft gentle breeze and and bright blue sky of spring. The conversation started as Harold had been walking past the parsonage and spotted Pastor Steve in the backyard chipping golf balls at a little sapling.

"Hi, slugger," Harold called. The pastor turned from the ball he was addressing. "Hi, Harold, come on back." The two men then hit several chip shots and talked casually. The pastor's wife brought iced tea out to the yard and they sat on lawn chairs. That's when it began. Harold had never told Steve about his war experiences. Steve only knew he had been a prisoner of the Japanese during World War II. In the pleasant sunshine of springtime, the two men were transported back through time and history to the mud and rain of the South Pacific.

"The first thing I remembered was being kicked out of bed. I was only half conscious and figured it was just the way we would be treated by our captors. When I came to enough to see, I realized it was a tall blond American in a tattered marine uniform. 'Bed' was a handful of straw and a woven mat."

He shouted, "Everybody out!" Harold sat back, lost in memory. "I had a 102° temperature. My leg was infected and I had a bullet in my shoulder. It turned out they were moving the entire camp and everyone that could get on their feet had to walk to the trucks. The marine captain who had jostled me was afraid that those who couldn't move might be left to die. We were close enough to the fighting to hear shots and explosions.

"I could barely remember my experiences from when I had been in the combat — I could remember we were being shelled. I didn't find out till many years later . . . a shell had hit the bunker and knocked me out breaking my leg. The bullet in my shoulder must have been a stray shot that hit me while I was down. I had been unconscious and two of my men carried me for several miles. They were captured. They took a wrong turn and had actually walked back of the enemy lines. A Japanese medic treated my wounds with first aid. The two men who brought me in tried to escape — one made it and the other was shot before he got under cover of the jungle. I had been semi-conscious for weeks. I didn't remember a thing.

"Anyway, the captain helped me up and we were loaded into trucks. Talking around I discovered some of the guys had been prisoners for months and some for just a few hours. The sounds of combat were all around us now. I wondered about escape myself. But breathing was almost too much effort.

"That night we were dumped by the roadside to sleep. In the morning we were loaded up again. By the afternoon of

61

the next day we were unloaded at an old base where engineers were stringing barbed wire and building watch towers. As we arrived there I had no idea that this camp would be my home for such a long time to come.

"We were a hopeless, helpless bunch when we arrived at what we called forever after, 'New Camp'. Everything was in chaos. The Japanese had little or nothing in the way of medical supplies or food. They were conscious of impending defeat and bitterly harsh with us prisoners. Some of the soldiers were in a state of panic and used their weapons on the prisoners more in frustration than out of cruelty. Some were just cruel. However, the Japanese were not our only problem. Our major problems were sickness and ourselves. Many of our men were physically ill. Fevers were common. Wounds were infected and ordinary things like headaches and dysentery were multiplied in pain and severity by our weakness and our lack of nourishment. Nothing seemed to go right. Latrines would fall apart. Men were obsessed with their own personal needs. Stealing was common. Fights among prisoners occurred often.

"The incident that changed things was the death of the marine captain. He had been one guy who had held up pretty well. When he came down with the fever, he refused medicine for himself and insisted it be given to others. When he died there were several men who owed him their life. Together they insisted on having a 'proper burial' for him. Burial details had been fairly routine up to that time. But not this time! Two of the men were British and one, an Episcopalian, had a Prayer Book with him. One of our men had a small American flag he had carried all this time.

"At the funeral service, the Prayer Book was passed around and several men read a portion of the service. At an appropriate time the flag was unfurled and laid across the box that the men had built for a coffin. Almost immediately the guards broke up the service and took away the flag. But three things had happened to us during the service. One — we had enlarged a good example of one man's expression of concern for others. That was enough to change some men on the spot. Second — we reclaimed a symbol of unity and of our heritage. The American flag could have been a British flag or Australian flag. Much later I realized that in an American prison camp it could have been a Japanese flag. But we reclaimed a sense of belonging and a pinch of pride in who we were. Third — the Prayer Book, or Book of Common Prayer, made us know for certain we were children of God and brothers. The lofty, austere words, so out of place in the prison camp, restored dignity to our shameful lives and strength in our failing weakness. The presence of God gave us order where there had been chaos and beauty where there had been only ugliness.

"Later that night some of the men asked the British soldier to have a religious service on Sunday. In trying to find out what day of the week it was, we discovered one of the guards was a Japanese Christian. Telling us which day was Sunday was only the first of many acts of Christian love that would come from his faith.

"We held services. We learned to pray, but more than that we learned to live and to help each other. Not everyone, and not all the time, but from that day on life was different. I figured when I got home I could leave my rifle, my uniform, and my faith behind me. They had served and served well. I wouldn't need any of them for peaceful civilian life.

"You know, it didn't work that way. My love for God was not just a wartime phenomenon. For weeks, for months, I couldn't figure out what was wrong. Then I bowed in prayer and from the first word I spoke I knew I'd discovered the problem. God is with us, not just 'in the Valley of the Shadow of Death' but even in the 'green pastures'. Some folks never figure that out. We have our faith stored up as a survival kit, rather than built up as a way of life."

Steve sat without speaking. Harold sipped his tea. The spring air circulated around them and they came back to an awareness of the sun and the green trees.

"That's quite a story, Harold." Steve was obviously moved by the experience.

Harold looked into the distance. "I think it helps me to tell it once in a while. Helps me to remember."

Steve got up from the lawn chair and picked up his pitching wedge. He pulled a golf ball into place. Then he looked at Harold. "It helped me, too!" and he hit the ball.

GETTING CLOSER TO GOD

Judy was ready to give it all up! "Forget it," she said, "the church is super dull." The only reason she had held on this long — she was 16 — was because of Pat, her girl friend, who always seemed to bounce in and out of church with enthusiasm and excitement. She figured her girl friend was just naturally enthusiastic.

One night, Judy mentioned her boredom to her friend. "I only go because my folks make me," she said, "I don't get anything out of it." But her friend surprised her with the words, "You aren't giving enough!" "Wait a minute!" Judy said, "I put a dollar a week in, just like you. That's a good part of my allowance!" "I know," said her friend, "but I'm talking about giving *yourself* during worship. I mean getting into the service — paying real attention to words and music — getting involved in the singing and the prayers and the sermon. It's not like going to the show or to a football game. Part of what happens in worship is what God makes happen and a big part is what *we* make happen. We have a share in it, each one of us. Otherwise it's nothing."

Judy seriously doubted her friend, but, out of friendship, she decided to try. She began coming early to church. She would take a seat and then take time to say a prayer. Judy wasn't much with words, but she would say things silently like, "God, I hope Pat is right — please help me worship. If this is important help me feel it, help me know it." Judy worked hard at trying to just forget everything else and think about God's Spirit. Sometimes the harder she tried the more irritated she felt and the more empty the service seemed. She would look around at the windows and the altar and cross. She tried to really see the people who were coming in to worship. She thought, "If everyone was like Pat, I could really enjoy coming to church." But then she realized . . . she hadn't tried to get to know the other people.

Judy concentrated on the music of the prelude and realized how spectacular it could be. Then, when the service started, she tried to take hold of every word, to grasp its meaning and feel its purpose. Sometimes minutes would go by and she would just be drifting. Then she would hear — really hear — a phrase or just a word. Then God's Spirit would touch her and the church would seem brighter.

During the sermon one Sunday, Judy got an idea — she prayed for God to help the pastor and guide him and she discovered she could hold tightly to the points the pastor made. It didn't work every time . . . but sometimes it was a miracle for her! She even scribbled notes on her worship bulletin from Sunday to Sunday. Once she jotted down a question for the pastor and once she wrote down a sentence from a sermon that fit a situation at school.

Judy told Pat one Sunday, "The big thing is the music. I can hardly believe it. Sometimes it's like God is reaching out to touch me." During the hymns, she would let herself go and sing out loud and clear. Judy was in the chorus at school but it just never dawned on her to sing that way in church. She began to feel the music as it surged and rolled and she took time to see the information about who wrote it and when. She reread some of the words and meaning emerged like seedlings pushing back the soil.

Judy still fidgets some Sundays and drifts now and then, but she said to Pat, "I think it's working. I really feel stronger and closer to God." Having discovered worship as a natural and universal experience, Judy quietly and almost unintentionally became an example for others. "My restlessness didn't come from dull worship alone. It was my own fault, too," she said to Bob, her boy friend. "You have to expect something to happen, then it can and will happen!"

GOD IS PRESENT NO MATTER WHERE

The giant jet circled in the clear sky surrounded by the blue that coined the name "Mediterranean blue." Mr. and Mrs. Hansen caught their first sight of Jerusalem from the air.

Allen Hansen, an electrical engineer, was flying to the Holy Land on a contracting job. His wife, Elly, had come along for the "pleasure" of being with her husband and because she'd ". . . always wanted to visit the Middle East."

It was ironic that the Hansen's first sight of the Holy City was fogged by a silly disagreement, a smoldering argument smothered by the public setting of the airplane, but still smoldering nonetheless. They were still angry with one another and not speaking to each other as the vista of the city swept into view below. The growing feeling of hostility between the Hansens over the last several years seemed to come from their discontent and frustration with life and family "in our middle age" as Elly would say. Their life seemed to lack meaning and direction. Their hope was that the time and travel together, the "pleasure," would help them to find themselves and one another. It obviously wasn't working!

68

Elly slammed the bathroom door. Driving from the airport to the hotel, Elly and Allen both refused to speak. Not a single word passed between them. The taxi driver pointed out ancient sights for them to see but the city flashed by distorted by their anger.

The next morning the sunshine coming in from the terrace was clouded by their continued feeling of conflict. Allen dressed and left for his first business meeting.

Elly sat on the bed. She started to cry. Then she said "no!" through her clenched teeth and slammed her fist into the pillow. She walked to the terrace and stepped outside. The temple dome glowed in the sun. The history of the city seemed to radiate from the buildings and the hills. The splendor made her even more angry. She gripped the rail and glared at the temple. Then she turned away. She went back into the hotel room. She dressed and went down to the lobby.

Her plan for the first day had been to meet two of the wives whose husbands were in Jerusalem on the same project. They were going to go shopping, but she didn't feel like facing other people today. She walked out of the hotel into the busy street. She walked down the street, hesitantly, looking into shop windows and watching the people.

Everyone seemed to be on their way to somewhere and in a hurry. She felt a desperate sense of drifting. She knew where she was but felt lost. She looked back up the street to the hotel. The city seemed like a whirl of confusion. The chaos drove her back toward the hotel entrance. The tour bus was sitting in the driveway as she reached the main doors of the hotel and she stopped. "I certainly don't feel like taking a tour with a canned lecture on historical religious locations." But she went to the desk in the lobby and asked about the tours.

She ridiculed herself as she boarded the bus. "This is silly. I hate tours like this." She settled into a seat by the window of the bus. "This is really silly," she said again.

Staring out the window, Elly came to when the guide's voice broadcast the words, "Jesus of Nazareth." She thought to herself, "These are the very streets where Jesus Christ walked." She sat back and began to daydream again. This time her thoughts had direction and purpose. The buildings and the stones of the streets sliding by seemed to give up their ghosts from the past. In her imagination Elly saw the cars and busses transformed into carts and donkeys. The people seemed to blur and then reappear in the costumes of ancient Jerusalem. Then she saw Jesus walking down the street toward the temple. Several men were walking with him. The busy crowds paid no attention to Jesus or the men.

In her mind's eye, she saw Him standing before the Roman Governor and the angry King Herod. She saw Him carrying His cross, bleeding from the wounds caused by the lash and the thorns. She wiped a tear from her eye. The great cross thudded against the pavement. Deep inside of her mind she asked herself, "What's happening to me?" It was as if she were walking through the crowds that jammed the streets. Now and then she caught a glimpse of the top of the cross or the head of Jesus grotesquely smeared with blood from the hard sharp thorns. On one occasion she seemed, for a moment, to catch His eye and the moment froze. In the rumbling confusion Jesus conveyed a message of calm, a feeling of trust, of one who knew the course of events and trusted the outcome while bearing the pain of the moment. She had drawn a deep breath as He looked at her. Her reaction, she realized now, had been one of surprise not one of shock. She had felt a warm surge of acceptance and sharing.

For the moment her imagination faded as reality returned to focus. The bus, the people, the sunshine, the noise and the tour guide . . . "departing in 15 minutes." People were getting up and stepping off the bus. She looked out the window but did not recognize the surroundings. As she stepped off she asked the guide where they were. He looked at her momentarily as if about to say something else and then said, "At the tomb."

Elly followed the other passengers. They went along the rocky path until they stood facing the open door of the tomb. The guide began to speak, "Here you see . . ."

Elly felt her imagination generating its own images again . . . The scene was hazy for an instant and then the clearing images revealed the great stone in place over the mouth of the tomb. Roman soldiers stood on guard. Elly wondered if they would notice her. Somehow in the back of her mind she knew they would not. As she watched, the scene, bathed in darkness, came alive with light. The soldiers stood for a moment at attention and then slumped forward in unison

71

as if asleep. The great stone trembled and rolled aside. Jesus stood in the door of the tomb. She saw Him bathed in light yet not in any spectacular way. She thought that the light seemed "appropriate." He looked from one side to the other. Then He looked at her. Elly wondered if He could see her. Somehow in the back of her mind she knew He could. Their eyes engaged and His face seemed to enlarge beyond the size of reality. Jesus spoke one word, "Peace." Then imagination and reality merged. Elly felt confusion and weakness. She blinked her eyes. She was in the sky with faces drifting around her. No, she was looking into the sky, the sun glaring down on her. The shadowy faces turned solid. They were vaguely familiar. One was a woman who had been sitting next to her on the bus. She thought, "What are you doing here?" Then reality was with her. "What am I doing here?" she heard herself say, as if from a distance.

"I'm sorry, ma'am, you fainted," said a tall man in the group. His wife nodded. Everyone looked worried. "Are you all right? Do you faint often? Where are you staying?" She shook her head, partly to answer their questions and partly to clear her thoughts. "What's happening to me?" she thought. "I'm okay," she said out loud. They helped her to the bus. Everyone seemed to care. Everyone was kind and concerned. As she sat on the bus riding back to the hotel, she felt calm, almost unconcerned. Her feeling was not casual. She felt "healthy," a healthy sense of life. She just felt good!

When she got back to the hotel she showered and changed her clothes. There was a Bible in the top drawer of the night stand "courtesy of the hotel." She took it from the drawer. Then she went out on the balcony and looked out over the city. The sun, now lower on the horizon, cast long dark shadows in contrast to bright orange highlights. Elly took the Bible and thumbed through the pages reading at random. She saw the words, "He is going before you to Galilee; there you will see Him as He told you." She read for quite a while. She hadn't prayed for years. Now she looked out over the ancient site and spoke, "God, I don't understand this. It's very real and yet so strange. It seems so reasonable to encounter Jesus and yet so impossible for me. I know I feel at home within myself and for Allen. I just never thought of receiving it like this. I don't know if this is religion, I only know that for me right now it's reality." The images of ancient Jerusalem and of Jesus' death and resurrection danced in her head. The implications to her and Allen and their life were staggering. Yet the joy she felt was comforting, giving her assurance and strength.

When Allen arrived at the hotel room, she was still on the balcony. He stood in the doorway for a few seconds. "Honey, I'm sorry about the plane ride and my stupid attitude, I . . ." She turned toward him and he stopped cold. She was smiling. She took his hand and they stepped to the balcony rail. He bent and kissed her softly. "Isn't it beautiful?" she said. But Allen was still looking at her. He said, "Elly, on our afternoon break one of the guys had a car and we drove around. Bill Freeman is a construction supervisor from one of the other contracting companies. He really knows the city and the Bible. Everything seemed so real here in one of the actual cities where Jesus was alive and active. I know we haven't thought seriously about religion or church since we were married and had our wedding service in the church. I felt so lousy and so much of what Bill said made sense. Well, I've been thinking. I hope you don't think I'm crazy, but maybe if we took God and religion more seriously things would be different. I don't see how it can hurt. I guess it sounds stupid."

Elly was smiling. She said, "I'm willing to try, Allen."

It didn't happen over night. But they talked that night and their love for one another was rekindled in the light and hope of Jesus Christ. Several years later, Elly said to her pastor, "I still don't know what happened that day. God communicated! I've certainly learned since then that I wouldn't have had to go clear to Jerusalem to find God through Jesus Christ. If only people would look and see, no matter where they are, God is present." When she said that, Allen laughed and added, "Sure He is. Why, He can even be present in two places at once."

A CHURCH OF THEIR OWN

When Jim left home, his mom and dad worried.

They had been good parents. With Jim and his little brother, "Tick", they were a good family with a strong standard of values and a strong home life. Together they were a "church-going family." Jim was accustomed to the example of his parents who often talked about their faith. Christianity was assumed to be a part of their life. They were intelligent and well-educated people. If Jim expressed doubts or asked questions, they seemed interested and understanding. But when Jim left home, they worried.

Back when Jim entered high school, he seemed to drift away from the values and priorities of his parents. "I just don't feel like doing homework," he would say. He never did anything wrong, he just did less and less that was right. He never rebelled against the Christian faith but grew increasingly indifferent.

During his junior year in high school, Jim was hospitalized with pneumonia and though his recovery was normal, he came away from the experience shaken and embittered. "I don't care" developed into a way of dealing with almost everything. He just drifted.

"I want to join the Army," Jim told his father one day. His father signed the papers because they hoped he would find something to interest him in the Army. He was stationed in North Carolina. His letters home were mostly requests for money and complaints about the conditions. He was transferred to California and he wrote less and less.

One Saturday morning his mother opened a thin envelope containing a single, small piece of stationery and a photograph. Jim said in the letter, "I got married Wednesday morning." The photograph was of a small blonde girl and on the back were the words, "This is Judy." Jim and Judy had married on short notice while Jim was on a three-day pass. The days and weeks went by and his mom and dad heard little or nothing. They never had an opportunity to meet Judy.

Now and then a letter arrived with a snapshot or two — mostly scenery — and one picture of the newlyweds. Jim's mother remarked to her husband, "Neither of them is smiling." The short letter said little or nothing except that the young couple had visited Los Angeles, or had been to the seashore, or crossed the desert to see the mountains. The parents were worried and hoped to travel to California to see their son and his wife. But that just never seemed possible.

One of Jim's letters, however, ended with the words, "God bless you!" The parents were momentarily surprised and puzzled, but they thought no more of it. In a subsequent letter, Jim said, referring to a sick army buddy, " . . . and we pray he will recover." When Jim had left for the Army, his mother had often pressed the issue of faith in Jesus Christ and her concern for Jim attending church, but as time passed, she had yielded to his indifference and had stopped expressing her worried thoughts.

Jim's father was startled to see his wife smiling and to see her blink back tears as she read the latest of Jim's letters. It was three pages long. Jim, now 22 years old, wrote of a small church that he and Judy had visited at the invitation of a friend on the base. Jim described the simple worship service and the friendliness of the people they met there. He said, "When we went back the next Sunday we were greeted like old friends." He commented on Judy's "church background" and the habit her folks had of going to church. "I guess we both just lost interest." Neither of them had talked much about it since marriage. Now suddenly religion was a fresh, new experience. Jim told his mom about the young minister coming to call on them at their apartment. Jim had finished working on the car and Judy was coming up from the laundry room in a robe and slippers. The three of them had coffee together and laughed about the look on Judy's face when she first saw the minister. Jim concluded the story by saying that now he and Judy had found "their own church."

The letter ended with these words, "Mom and Dad, maybe you think I will crack-up or lose a few marbles if something goes wrong or if we have difficulty. Don't worry, that will never happen now. You think I was strong before — well, maybe — but that is nothing to the strength we have now since we've found the place for the church in our lives."

NURSE'S AIDE

"The doctor said he'll meet us at the hospital!" Mrs. Johnson was frightened. Her husband, Fred, said, "Everything's going to be all right, Frances."

The Johnsons put their two daughters, Janie 10 and Melissa 12, into the car and left for the hospital. Both girls were running high fevers and had been extremely ill during the night. Mrs. Johnson kept repeating, "Hurry, Fred, hurry."

Doctor Schmidt was in the Emergency Room when they arrived. The parents sat down, relieved, as the doctor took over. After a thorough examination of the girls, Doctor Schmidt came back to the Johnsons and said, "Both girls are resting quietly now. The virus hit them hard." He told the parents they could stay with the girls for the night. "We need to watch their temperature very carefully."

As the couple entered the hospital room, they went directly to their daughters' beds. Neither paid any attention to the black woman in a nurse's aide uniform who was just tucking the sheet on Janie's bed. When the doctor turned to leave he said, "Mr. and Mrs. Johnson, this is Florence. She's going to stay nearby and check the girls frequently tonight.

On this floor Florence is my boss. Florence Packston, this is Mr. and Mrs. Johnson."

The Johnsons saw her for the first time. In spite of their worry over their daughters, they reacted visibly to her. The Johnsons had been Christians all their lives. They believed in human equality and the brotherhood of humanity, or at least they thought they did. But in the city, they were, according to Fred, " . . . run out of the neighborhood." The Johnsons had moved out to Maryville, Fred said, "to get away from 'them'." He often said, "If they move within 10 miles of us, we'll move again!"

Now he stood staring at the black woman. She extended her hand toward him but now her hand faltered and then dropped to her side. She smiled. She said, "Janie and Melissa are going to be fine. You both make yourselves comfortable. I'll be here if you need me." Mr. Johnson mumbled, "Thank you," and then turned back to the girls.

The night was a blur. Time passed heavily. The darkened hospital room with the dim night light near the floor invited sleep. The frantic rush as the girls became violently ill forbade the possibility of real sleep. The cadence of their labored breathing as they slept touched the parents with concern. Through all the blur, Florence Packston moved with gentle authority. She repeatedly cradled one or the other of the girls in her arms. She walked with them as they shuffled sleepily to and from the bathroom. She spoke in quiet words of soothing sweetness when they cried. From time to time, her soft quiet laughter would brighten the darkness.

Mrs. Johnson awoke once and realized there was a pillow under her head and a blanket over her. Mr. Johnson felt a tap on his arm, as he stared out the window at the night sky, and turned to see Florence, who was handing him a cup of coffee. He started to speak, but she heard Melissa mumble something and went immediately to the bedside.

Twice during the night, Mrs. Johnson heard a whispered prayer from the lips of the nurse's aide.

Morning broke with sunshine in a bright blue sky. The girls' fever had broken in the quiet hours of the morning. The Johnsons kissed each of the sleeping girls. "Thank you, Lord, for life and hope," they said.

As they left, Frances Johnson put her arms around Florence Packston and said, "God bless you." Mr. Johnson took the nurse's aide by the hand, covering her hand with both of his. He looked at her and said, "Thank you." Then, with great difficulty, he said very quietly, "I'm sorry!"

THE DOCTOR'S DREAM

Cindy sat at the reception desk in the lobby of the medical building. "So long, Cindy! Thank God it's Friday. Will you be in tomorrow?" the doctor asked. "No, Pauline will be here tomorrow, doctor."

"Boy, I'm glad Saturday is only a half-day. Have a nice weekend, Cindy!" The doctor put on his sport coat and went through the lobby out onto the sidewalk.

"Try to get some rest, Doctor Paulsen." Cindy waved as he went by and then returned her attention to the phone panel. She knew from experience that the half-day coming up tomorrow would start early and end late. She shook her head. "I sure hope he can get by the weekend without any emergency calls."

The scene and the concerns repeated themselves when the doctor left the building two and a half hours late on Saturday. At the reception desk, Pauline said, "Have a pleasant weekend, doctor!"

If Pauline or Cindy could have followed Doctor Paulsen

when he left the office and after he stopped to have a sandwich at the delicatessen, they would have been surprised to see him turn up the ramp to the expressway that went through the quiet suburb where the doctor's office is located. They would have been doubly surprised to see him turn toward the open country and away from the neighboring suburb where he lived.

Harry Paulsen had sixty miles to drive in order to reach the little town of Leaberg. He had made the trip now for nearly a year. He goes every third weekend. He and two other doctors make the trip alternately, one of them each weekend.

In order to explain the trips, Harry would have to go back to the last summer when he and his wife and two sons were on vacation. That's where he started the story when he told it to his two colleagues, Doctor Jones and Doctor Pawchoski. When they heard his story, they agreed to work with him on his plan — or, as he called it, "my dream."

On a Saturday evening, the Paulsens were returning from a two-week camping trip and coming through Leaberg they were relaxed, pleasantly tired and eager to get home, get cleaned up and sleep in their own beds. Talking about their feelings, Harry Paulsen had just said, "There's nothing like your own bed and clean sheets after a camping trip." There was a terrible sound of grinding metal and the bumping of parts of the car that were not supposed to bump. Harry pulled off the road immediately and there before them was a little country filling station. In the window was a hand-lettered sign that said "Mechanic on Duty." "From the looks of the sign, he's been on duty for a long time," Harry said to his wife. They got out of the car and walked into the station.

Two hours later they were checking into the motel in the town. The mechanic had diagnosed the trouble — a broken axle — and they decided to stay over night. The motel was a small, privately-owned motel. "At least the sheets are clean, Dad," one of his sons remarked. The mechanic had said he'd have his brother bring the parts with him from the city, where he worked nights. "And, right after church, I'll get to work and have you on the road in no time."

In the morning, Harry and his family had breakfast at the little diner next to the motel. People were friendly and had apparently heard of their car trouble. They went to the church down the street. They went partly because folks in the diner, in the motel and at the filling station had talked about church and invited them, and partly because they regularly attended church when they were home. Harry often said, "Thank God we have more to count on and to have faith in than our human knowledge and skill." He was an extremely competent physician but often noted, "I've never touched a patient without praying for God's help."

At the little village church, Harry and his family enjoyed the simple service of worship and the elderly pastor's sermon. He had spoken lovingly of God's creation and the glories of nature and the words fit with with their recent camping experience. Following church, two couples invited them to Sunday dinner after they had accepted the invitation of the couple who sat beside them at worship.

The folks were all standing outside the church on the lawn and by the street when a dusty pick-up truck came tearing down the street at high speed and skidded to a stop in front of the church. The young man who hopped out spoke with a Spanish accent as he asked the pastor to help him locate "Mr. and Mrs. Ferrer."

The doctor had noticed with approval that there were a number of families at worship who were of Mexican descent. He assumed they lived in the area. Mr. and Mrs. Ferrer came right past him as they rushed to their car. She was crying and obviously something was wrong.

Doctor Paulsen stepped forward and said, "Excuse me, I'm a doctor. Can I help?" The pastor nodded, "You sure can. They've sent a man to Carlton to try to get an ambulance but that will take more than an hour at best. Their son fell from the tractor seat and was caught by the wheels of the tractor and then hit his head on a stone. He is alive, but unconscious. They were afraid to move him." All the time they talked the pastor had propelled the doctor toward the waiting car with a strong hand on his shoulder. They sped to the farm with the young man following in the beat-up pick-up truck.

On the way there the doctor learned that these people were farm workers and that the church in town had developed a new ministry of concern for them. The boy who had fallen was only 12 years old. He and his brothers had stayed home from church that day in order to complete additional chores that had been prevented by rain.

Arriving at the scene, Doctor Paulsen examined the boy and then supervised moving him into the house. There he was able to treat the boy with those things he always carried when they went camping. He chuckled inwardly because his wife always said, "You look more like we're going to a disaster than on a vacation the way you pack that medical bag." But she would laugh and he would always take it along.

By the time the ambulance from Carlton arrived, they had little to do but put the boy in the vehicle and leave. But Doctor Paulsen had had plenty of time to talk with the family of the boy and the family that owned the farm. His "dream" was born even before he left that farm house.

Using his own money, he established a weekend clinic in a store front in town. He soon discovered that he couldn't go to Leaberg every weekend nor could he be of much help if he only went once or twice a month. So he talked to the other two doctors he had known since medical school. They each agreed to take charge of a weekend. They sought help from the town's people and farmers and even secured a grant from a foundation. But the biggest boost came from the school children who planned a big carnival in the church-yard with ring toss and water balloon toss and popcorn to eat. The doctors worked at developing a comprehensive health program for the farm workers. "Preventive medicine will make the job of the clinic possible," Doctor Paulsen said.

"I had to explain to my minister why one of his deacons and regular ushers at the Sunday services was absent so much." He told me, "Professionally you may be a doctor, but you're enough of a theologian to know that service such as you are doing is worship and that what you do for the people of Leaberg is what you are doing for Jesus Christ. Besides, Harry, the Men's Chorus has been on key since you left it to minister to the people of Leaberg!" The minister had laughed then — and Harry laughed as he recalled the words.

Harry Paulsen was a quiet man with a gentle sense of humor and few people beside his wife and minister knew of this effort. "The people of Leaberg know and that's enough for Harry," his wife said.

THE STILL SMALL VOICE

Death had come peacefully and quietly for Marion. Her whole life had been one of quiet peace. She had filled it with deeds of kindness and soft-spoken words of encouragement to others. Few would think of her now as a person who had proclaimed the faith of Christ, nor would she be long-remembered as a woman who presented God's spirit to the world.

The paradox of Marion's life is that her story begins with her death, for she found in God and His Spirit the cause and purpose for which she lived. She did not seek to be known by others and she was not widely known. She sought instead to know people, a few people. She sought to know them well and to know them in the context of Jesus Christ and His Gospel. She was not a teacher or a writer. She had lived and worked for her 76 years within her home and family. People in the church and the community often said, "Marion is always there when you need her." She was known as a "quiet person." It would be safe to say she was truly a humble person.

In her life the power of God rested in simple acceptance. Few would have questioned Marion's faith, yet very few, if any, ever thought of her faith as a lively and active factor for her or for others. She is one of the "still small voices" that speak the Gospel. They utter the Word of God during the din and roar of life and, though they seem to be so easily shouted down and overwhelmed, they go on speaking and somehow again and again the voice is heard and needed.

Marion left four written lines in the beautiful scripted longhand taught long ago in grade schools and inscribed with a quill-type pen. It is on a yellowed card written when she was very young and carried with her through most of life. The words are not in quotations and bear no author's name. She may have written them herself,

Lord, lay some soul upon my
heart, and love that soul
through me, and may I nobly do
my part to bring that soul to Thee.

She was a quiet saint of God — unknown, unheralded and unrewarded, save in the sight of God. And that seems to be all the reward or notice such people seem to need.